KW-053-442

Human Rights

CLEAN ENVIRONMENT

CENTRAL REGIONAL SCHOOL LIBRARY SERVICE

SARA JONES

Wayland

Titles in the Human Rights series
Clean Environment
Food
Freedom of Expression
Homeland
Justice
Shelter

Cover illustrations: *background* The roads of Los Angeles, California at dusk. Look how the air is thick with pollution; *inset* The beautiful Atlantic rainforest with cassia and tibouchina trees in bloom in Sierra Dos Orgaos, Brazil.

2111506OG

Copy No.   1

Class No.   333.7

Author   JON

First published in 1993 by
Wayland (Publishers) Ltd

61 Western Road, Hove
East Sussex BN3 1JD
England
© Copyright 1993 Wayland (Publishers) Ltd

Editor: Deborah Elliott
Designer: Joyce Chester
Picture editor: Geraldine Nicholls

British Cataloguing in Publication Data
Jones, Sara
Clean Environment. – (Human rights)
I. Title II. Series
333.7
ISBN 0-7502-0834-1

Picture acknowledgements

Bruce Coleman Limited cover inset (Luiz Claudio Marigo), 40 (Nicholas De Vore); ECOSCENE 9, 10 (Cooper), 24 (Cooper), 25 (Gryniewiecz), 36 (Adrian Morgan); Environmental Picture Library 8, 19 (H. Girardet), 21 (Chris Rose); Eye Ubiquitous 38 (Julia Waterlow); Greenpeace 14 (Lambon), 28 (Merjenburgh), 29 (Terry Bush); G.S.F. Picture Library 6, 13, 27; Hutchison Library 22, 35 (Bernard Regent); Impact 33 (Sergio Dorantes), 39 (Colin Jones), 44 (Jonathan Pile); NHPA 26 (Peter Johnson); Oxfam 23 (Jeremy Hartley); Photri 16 (Dennis MacDonald); Popperfoto 12 (Reuter); Quadrant 43 (Wagner); Science Photo Library 4 (European Space Agency), 17 (NASA, Goddard Institute for Space Studies), 20 (NASA/GSFC); Tony Stone Worldwide cover background (Ken Biggs), 18 (Glen Allison), 31 (John Warden), 34 (Julian Calder), 37 (David Paterson), 41 (Stephen Studd); Topham Picture Library 11; Wayland Picture Library 30, 95; ZEFA 5, 32.

Contents

1

The price of progress

THE environment is your whole world. It is the air you breathe, the water you drink, the buildings you live in, and the transport you use. It is somewhere you expect to feel safe.

Whenever we have found our environment threatening, we have found ways to overcome the dangers. We built shelters to fend off attacks from wild animals. We developed heating systems to keep us warm in cold climates. We discovered medicines to cure diseases. As time has passed, our ways of beating, taming and shaping the environment have become more sophisticated. Now, the industrial world's environment could be said to have been licked into shape. We have heat, light and water at the click of a switch and the turn of a tap. We can travel to any city or country in the world. For most of the people in developed countries, such as Europe, Australia, Canada and the USA, life can be very comfortable.

However, these advances, which have made our lives not only more comfortable, but healthier and longer than in previous generations, have had other, less welcome effects on our environment. For example, burning coal, oil and gas (fossil fuels) in power stations, cars and other vehicles, causes global warming. Some environmentalists believe that global warming is the most serious threat facing humanity around the world today.

The Earth is extremely precious. It supports many life forms and has places of exceptional beauty. We must protect the Earth.
This image shows Africa, Europe, the Middle East and part of South America.

When fossil fuels are burned they produce the so-called greenhouse gases, the most important being carbon dioxide. The Earth is warmed by heat from the Sun. This heat escapes slowly into space. However, the greenhouse gases stop heat from escaping. The gases act like glass in a greenhouse. So, the Earth is getting warmer.

The more greenhouse gases we produce the hotter the Earth becomes. The problem is made worse by the destruction of the tropical rainforests. Plants and trees absorb (soak up) carbon dioxide. The rainforests have the greatest concentration of plants in the world. The fewer trees there are, the less carbon dioxide is absorbed and the temperature rises.

Glaciers descending from the polar ice-caps. If temperatures continue to rise, the ice-caps could melt, causing flooding.

Over the last 100 years, the average global surface-air temperature has risen by around 0.5°C. The hottest six years on record occurred between 1981 and 1991. By the middle of the next century, the world could be 1.5°C hotter than it is now.

Scientists are still not sure precisely what effects global warming will have. But a change of just 2-3°C could melt the polar ice-caps. This may cause the level of the seas to rise, which could cause severe flooding. Dry parts of the world could experience terrible droughts, causing widespread famine.

Can you see how this coniferous forest in Bayerisherwald, on the border of Germany and Czechoslovakia, has been damaged by acid rain? The acid rain was caused by pollution from power stations.

We have caused other serious environmental problems. Smoke from power stations and factory chimneys contains a chemical called sulphur. Sulphur pollutes moisture in the air. The polluted moisture falls to the ground as rain or snow, called acid rain. Acid rain is killing fish and forests, and destroying the stonework of buildings.

The use of chemicals called chlorofluorocarbons (CFCs) in household appliances, such as aerosols and refrigerators, has destroyed much of the ozone layer. Ozone is a layer of gas in the stratosphere – about 10-15 km above the surface of the Earth. The ozone layer protects us from the harmful effects of the Sun's rays.

Many farmers spray their crops with pesticides to kill any insects living on them. However, the pesticides contain chemicals which can be harmful to humans and animals if they get into the food chain. Pesticides can also be washed by rain into rivers and streams, polluting our water.

The list of environmental problems seems to be endless. It seems that just by living we are polluting the Earth.

What are we to do? We all want the comforts that modern industrialized societies have to offer, but we also want clean air, water and food. Obviously some kind of balance must be struck.

People who belong to the green movement believe that having a comfortable life should not mean simply everyone being able to own a dishwasher, a car, a television, central heating and air-conditioning, but that everyone should be able to breathe clean air, drink pure water, and enjoy the countryside too. They want to make sure that the Earth will be just as comfortable for future generations.

In fact, there are no laws which give us any rights to a safe, clean environment. The United Nations (UN) is the meeting place for representatives of all the world's governments. In 1948, members of the UN drew up a set of rules on human rights by which all peoples can live together peacefully and fairly without injustice and inequality. This set of rules was called the 'Universal Declaration of Human Rights'. The 'Declaration' gives us the right to things such as freedom of speech and of religion, but not to a safe, healthy environment.

All over the world, environmental pressure groups have sprung up to try to make sure that we are given some rights. They want governments to take action to cut down our consumption of the Earth's resources. Indeed, almost every country in the world is now passing laws which aim to protect the environment.

Governments have also recognized that the environmental problems are international and need international solutions. Groups of scientists and ministers from all over the world meet regularly to discuss what should be done about environmental issues. Over the past few years, we have had the United Nations' Intergovernmental Panel on Climate Change, the Ramsar Convention to protect the Wetlands, the Geneva Convention on Air Pollution, the Convention on International Trade in Endangered Species (CITES), and the World Summit held in Rio de Janeiro in 1992.

The World Conservation Union, the Organization for Economic Co-operation and Development (OECD) and the United Nations Environment Programme co-ordinate, develop and monitor environmental policies.

The World Health Organization (WHO) draws up standards for countries to follow on topics such as air pollution, and seas and rivers. Often these guidelines will form part of a country's own legislation (laws). Often, too, the guidelines are completely ignored. The only organization whose decisions have to be enforced is the European Commission.

US politician Al Gore (front) addresses the World Summit in Rio de Janeiro. Beside him are two Indian chiefs, anxious to preserve the safety of the rainforests.

As individual countries develop their environmental policies, their citizens are gaining some rights. One of these is the right to know what makes up the items we buy. Many countries now force companies to 'eco-label' their products to show how environmentally friendly they are. But eco-labelling is by no means foolproof and many companies deliberately make their labelling unclear. For example, some plastics have been labelled as 'biodegradable'. This suggests the plastics will break down (decompose) into carbon dioxide and water when they are put in the earth. They do not. Plastics made of starch do decompose more quickly than ordinary plastics. However, it still takes years and they take more energy to make, and are less hard-wearing than ordinary plastics.

Nevertheless, gradually the loopholes in the labelling laws are being tightened. The more optimistic environmentalists think more rights will come our way, both as a result of pressure from people and because of political changes in the world. Author Lester R Brown sums up changing attitudes: 'The world's agenda will be more ecological than ideological, dominated less by relationships among nations and more by the relationship between nations and nature . . . All societies have an interest in satisfying the needs of the current generation without compromising the ability of future generations to meet their needs. It is in the interests of everyone to protect the Earth's life-support systems, for we all have a stake in the future habitability of the planet.'

2

Clean air

AIR is the most basic need of living creatures. Yet we are allowing it to become so polluted that, at certain times, people in cities such as Prague, Warsaw and Los Angeles, are advised not to go outdoors. Trees and fish are dying because of air-borne pollution and our climate is being affected.

In the USA, air pollution is believed to be reducing crop production by 10-15 per cent.

Nowadays, cyclists wearing face masks can be seen in most cities in the world. The masks protect cyclists from pollutants in vehicle exhausts.

Cars are the main cause of air pollution. There are 400 million cars in the world, 80 per cent of them in industrialized countries. Every year 19 million more cars are built. By 2025 there could be 1,000 million cars on our roads. Car engines give off pollutants, such as carbon dioxide, carbon monoxide, hydrocarbons and nitrogen oxides. These can be extremely harmful, not only to the atmosphere by contributing to global warming, but also to people's health. Every car produces

Filling up a car with unleaded petrol. Many people around the world now use unleaded petrol.

four times its own weight in carbon dioxide a year. Fumes from petrol that contains lead (leaded) can cause brain damage in children.

It is not only car engines that cause pollution. The actual process of building a car creates a large amount of carbon dioxide. Car seating is made of chlorofluorocarbons, which destroy the ozone layer. Asbestos, a powerful carcinogen (causes cancer), is used in the brake linings.

Some governments have taken steps to curb the amount of harmful chemicals a car can produce. Lead was first added to petrol in the 1920s to extend the life of exhaust valves. When it became clear just how dangerous lead could be, many countries acted to cut down its use. In 1985, the Swedish government ruled that every petrol station had to provide unleaded petrol. Within a year, two-thirds of Swedes whose cars could take unleaded petrol were doing so. Many other countries have since followed suit.

A three-way catalytic converter, a kind of filter, fitted to a car's exhaust can dramatically reduce the amount of nitrogen, hydrocarbons and carbon monoxide the car gives off. The exhaust fumes then contain nitrogen, water vapour and carbon dioxide. A two-way catalytic converter will help clean up hydrocarbons and carbon monoxide from a diesel engine.

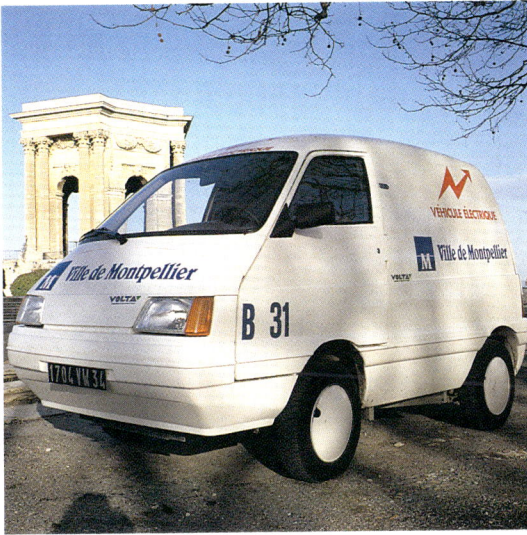

A vehicle that runs on electricity in Montpellier, France. Electric cars are environmentally friendly, but are not popular with drivers because they are not as fast or powerful as cars fuelled by petrol.

Germany and Sweden, among others, offer tax incentives to the buyers of cars with catalytic converters. In the USA, manufacturers have, by law, to fit catalytic converters to all new models. The amount of carbon dioxide produced by a car depends on how much fuel is burned. Some new models now use only half the amount of fuel used by older models.

Another way of reducing pollution from road vehicles is to develop a fuel other than petrol. The electric car has been around for many years but is not yet fast or powerful enough to attract many buyers. Brazil and Zimbabwe lead the world in the use of ethanol (ethyl alcohol) mixed with petrol, which reduces the amount of toxic (poisonous) fumes from car engines. There are also plans to produce a hydrogen-powered car by the end of the twentieth century.

Another option is to reduce the number of cars on the road by increasing the use of public transport (see chapter 5). The only problem is that most public transport uses diesel fuel. This produces high levels of carbon monoxide and particulates (tiny particles of carbon), which are also harmful to the environment.

Cars are not the only cause of air pollution. Industry is also a culprit. Sometimes industrial pollution is accidental. In December 1984, a leak from a chemical storage tank at a pesticides factory in the Indian town of Bhopal caused a fog of toxic fumes to sweep through the town. At least 2,000 people died and 200,000 more were injured. Many people suffered blindness or breathing, sleeping and eating disorders.

Bhopal was the scene of the worst industrial accident in history, but there have been many others with only slightly lower death tolls. The effects of accidents on the environment, however, are usually localized and not very long-lasting. What makes a much worse impact on the planet is the day-to-day running of industry.

Victims of the Bhopal disaster await judgement on the settlement of a compensation trial by India against the US owners of the pesticide factory responsible for the gas leak.

For years people looked to factories to provide jobs and livelihoods. But silently, invisibly, these factories poured out substances which killed or injured not only workers but people living nearby. Factories making or using asbestos, for example, were filling the air with tiny particles of the substance which we now know causes asbestosis, a particularly dangerous form of cancer.

The Katowice area of Poland is one of the most polluted places in the world. It produces one-third of Poland's coke, half its steel and almost all its coal. The country's lead and zinc is also processed in Katowice. Lech Zinn is a fifty-year-old miner from Katowice. 'I had to give up work because of the damage the coal dust did to my lungs. I have seen steeples fall off churches, eaten away by acid rain. I cannot eat the vegetables from my garden because the soil is polluted by lead and cadmium. Many of my friends have died from lung disease and cancer, caused by pollution from the factories.' Lech has reason to be concerned. The people of Katowice are twice as likely to die in their thirties as people elsewhere in Poland.

People started to realize the full dangers of industrial pollution about forty years ago. They decided to build factories with higher chimneys. Although this cleared many of the fumes from the immediate neighbourhood, it resulted in the pollution being carried many, often thousands, of kilometres away.

The effects of this were first noticed in Scandinavia (Norway, Sweden, Denmark, Finland, Iceland) in the 1960s. Large numbers of fish in rivers and lakes were dying. Then hundreds of trees in the picturesque Black Forest in Germany were found to be diseased and dying. By 1980, scientists had pin-pointed the culprits – sulphur dioxide and nitrogen oxide – and the source – the coal-fired power stations of Britain and Eastern Europe. Gases were being pumped high into the atmosphere, where they turned into acid and were carried thousands of kilometres before falling as rain, snow or fog. The countries which produce acid rain are rarely the countries that suffer the effects.

Heavy, black smoke, thick with pollutants is pumped out of power stations in Britain and Eastern Europe. Sulphur from the smoke turns moisture in the air acid. The polluted moisture falls to the ground as acid rain, snow or fog, damaging trees and buildings.

The problem is now so bad that 13,000 sq km of lakes and rivers in southern Norway are dead or dying. The seven most important salmon rivers in Norway have lost almost all their fish. In Sweden, 20,000 of the country's 100,000 lakes are now empty of fish. In the USA, brook trout are dying in the streams of the Adirondack Mountains. In Canada, the damage to maple trees from acid rain is threatening the country's profitable maple syrup industry.

Factories and power stations in Europe and North America pump out 100 million tonnes of sulphur dioxide into the atmosphere every year. There are special filters which can be fitted to the chimneys of coal-fired power stations. These filters take out the poisonous gases. However, they are very expensive and many companies are unwilling or unable to spend the money. There have been some international attempts to fight the pollution. In 1983, the United Nations Economic Commission for Europe called for reductions in sulphur dioxide in factories. Two years later, twenty-one countries agreed to reduce sulphur dioxide by one-third by 1993, and to freeze the levels of nitrogen oxides. But it looks as though many countries will not meet these targets and further negotiations are going on all over Europe.

One way to avoid acid rain is to stop using coal to make electricity. Alternative energy sources, such as power from the wind, Sun and water, do not produce sulphur dioxide or nitrogen oxide (see chapter 3).

The reactor at the nuclear power station in Chernobyl, the Ukraine, in which the disastrous explosion occurred in 1986. Nuclear pollution, caused by the explosion, spread across much of northern Europe.

Nuclear power does not produce acid rain. But environmentalists believe that nuclear power stations produce an even worse pollution – radiation. The most serious example of nuclear pollution was caused by the explosion at the nuclear plant in Chernobyl, in the Ukraine, in 1986. Radiation spread across what was then the USSR, into Scandinavia and northern Europe. Although not many people died at the time of the accident, many more have died since of radiation sickness. No one knows how many will die in years to come from cancer caused by radioactive fall-out. People living in towns in the Chernobyl area had to leave their homes, never to return. Crops and livestock in all the affected countries had to be destroyed.

Air pollution in our homes

Scientists have proved that the air in homes and buildings can be more seriously polluted than outdoor air, even in the largest and most industrialized cities.

The pollutants in our homes include asbestos, formaldehyde from various wood products and aerosols, paradichlorbenzene from mothballs and air fresheners, airborne pesticide residues, perchloroethylene from dry cleaning, and many other equally poisonous substances.

One of the most dangerous pollutants in our homes is a gas which is produced naturally. It has no smell or colour and is extremely radioactive. It is called radon and it seeps through the soil and collects in the lower storeys of buildings. In the USA, radon is second only to tobacco smoke as a cause of lung cancer.

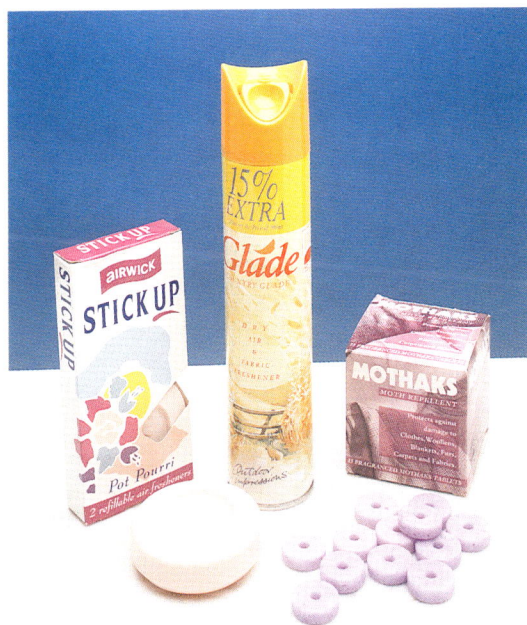

Danger lurks in our homes! Moth balls and air fresheners are common items found in most homes. Although they may appear to be useful products, in fact they contain chemicals which are extremely harmful to the environment.

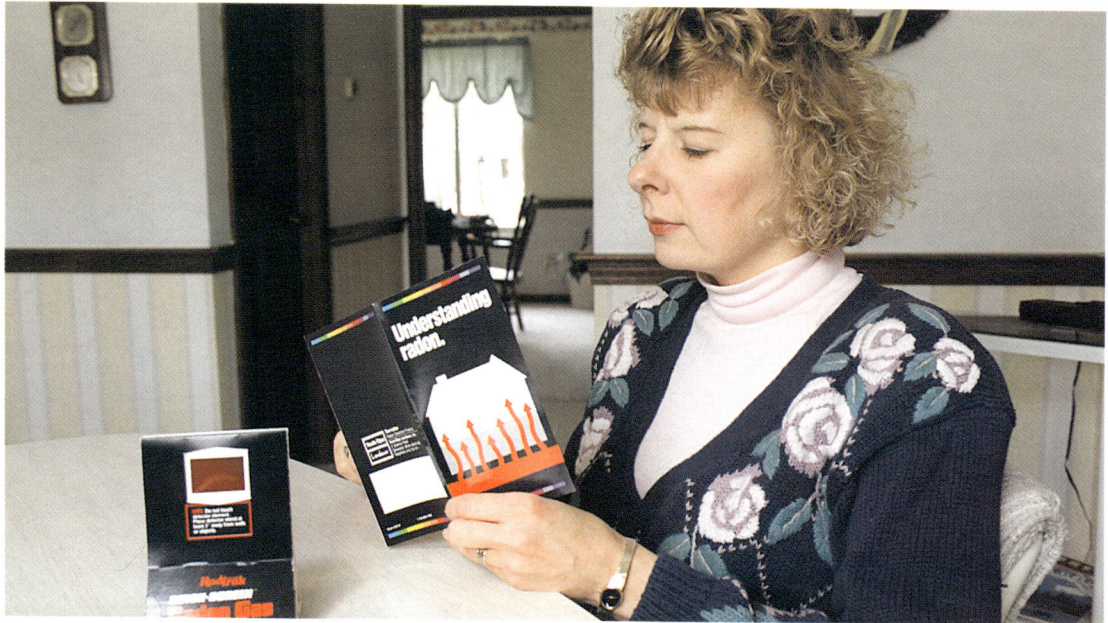

In 1988, the US Surgeon General recommended that all Americans living on the first floor or below should test their homes for radon. Homes with high radon levels can be treated. A good ventilation system helps prevent it building up.

It seems as though the quality of our air is under threat from all quarters: roads, industry, our homes, and even from nature itself. There have been some attempts to clean up our air. In 1987, the World Health Organization (WHO) drew together a panel of 130 experts from Europe and North America to set out guidelines on various air pollutants. Many countries fail regularly to match up to the standards required to improve air quality. Other countries, such as Japan, Switzerland,

Checking for radon gases in the home. Radon is an extremely radioactive gas which can cause lung cancer.

the Netherlands, France, and the USA, have strict air quality standards, sometimes more strict than the WHO guidelines. Governments of the USA, Japan, Germany, the Netherlands, France, Sweden and Denmark can issue pollution alerts. These give them the power to restrict the use of cars and to force factories to cut down the amount of gases they give off until the air clears.

Until more countries follow this lead, and everyone puts the needs of the atmosphere before those of the motorist and industry, our air will continue to be in pretty bad shape.

3

A healthy climate

PARTS of the Earth are very cold, while other parts are unbearably hot. Humans have had to develop ways of combatting the climate in order to survive. Unfortunately, many of these ways are harmful to the environment.

Since 1980, the world's temperature has risen by 0.5°C. Scientists are not sure whether this is due to the natural factors which affect climate, such as the Earth's orbit round the Sun, or whether it is because of greenhouse gases which are warming up the Earth.

The Intergovernmental Panel on Climate Change is looking into the problem of global warming, and a 'Treaty on Atmosphere' is hoped for soon. However, the signs are that the worst offenders are the least willing to

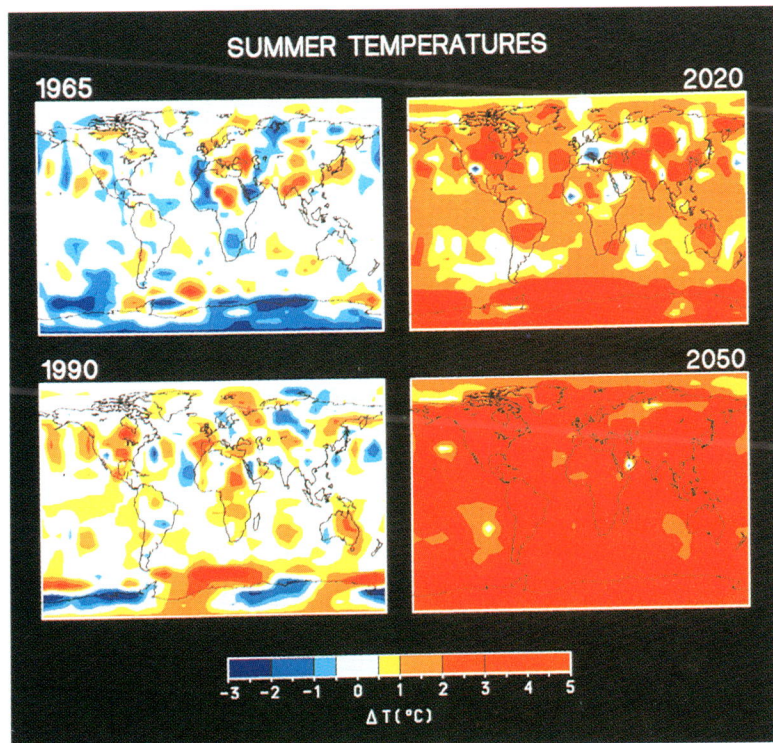

These computer-generated images of the world show how much the surface air temperatures have increased since 1965, and by how much they may increase by the year 2050. Red and orange indicate increased temperatures.

reduce emissions (amounts given out) of carbon dioxide. The UK has said it will reduce its emissions to their 1990 levels, but only if other countries will do so too. The US government has refused to do even this, saying it needs to be convinced that global warming is a real rather than an assumed threat.

Even if greenhouse gas production remained at present levels, the world's temperature might rise by about 0.2°C every decade for the next few decades.

These turbines are part of a wind farm in California, USA. The turbines are powered by energy from the wind. They, in turn, power generators which make electricity. Wind power is a clean and safe form of alternative energy.

This is because we are pumping out far more gases than the forests and oceans can absorb.

A good way of cutting carbon dioxide levels is by changing the ways we use and produce energy. At the moment, about three-quarters of the world's energy is produced by fossil fuels, which are not only running out, but are harming our environment too. If we used alternative energy sources, such as the Sun, the wind, or biofuel (waste matter that can be burned to produce energy), the amount of carbon dioxide given off would virtually disappear. Hydroelectric (power from water) schemes do not add to global warming but harm the environment in other ways (see chapter 7).

Until such time as governments commit themselves to using alternative energy supplies, there are ways in which we can cut down the amount of energy we use. Between 60 per cent and 80 per cent of energy used in homes is for heating. This can be reduced dramatically if buildings are properly insulated. Keeping a new house warm in Sweden uses less than one-third of the energy needed to heat a home in the UK. The 'superinsulated' homes in Sweden have triple- or even quadruple-glazing, and indoor shutters which cut down the heat loss from windows at night. The houses also have ventilation systems which recover heat from expelled air to warm up incoming fresh air. These 'super-insulated' houses can also be found in parts of Canada and the northern states of the USA.

Many fossil fuel-fired power stations waste huge amounts of energy. When coal or oil is being turned into electricity, the waste comes out as steam, escaping into the atmosphere through huge cooling towers. In Germany and parts of Scandinavia, this steam is used to heat hospitals and factories through a system called Combined Heat and Power (CHP). A power station with a CHP system uses half the amount of fuel to produce the same amount of energy as a conventional fossil fuel-fired power station.

Tropical rainforests absorb huge amounts of carbon dioxide. However, the rainforests are gradually being destroyed by developers.

There is another very important step that must be taken if we are to save our climate from global warming. We must protect the world's forests. Plants and trees act as 'sinks', absorbing huge amounts of carbon dioxide. The tropical rainforests, which are vast and extremely dense, are vitally important for this task. They have been called 'the lungs of the world'. Yet, in the last forty years, about half the world's tropical forests have been cut down (see chapter 7). It is extremely important that the forests are protected and new trees planted.

Road traffic is another source of greenhouse gases. Far fewer vehicles running more cleanly and efficiently would greatly reduce the amount of carbon dioxide pumped out into the atmosphere.

So far we have looked at how we keep warm in cold climates. We have also found ways of keeping cool in hot climates. Air-conditioning systems have made life tolerable for many people in extremely hot cities. But air-conditioning systems not only use a lot of electricity, but they also require chemicals called chlorofluorocarbons (CFCs). CFCs and HCFCs (hydro-chlorofluorocarbons) are used in aerosols, blowing agents for types of foam used in seating and for packing supermarket goods, and glues and cleaning fluids used in industry. One-third of CFCs and HCFCs are used in refrigeration systems, including domestic fridges and air-conditioning.

The problem with CFCs is that they destroy the ozone layer. CFCs and some other gases, such as halons used in fire extinguishers, do not break down in the lower atmosphere. They travel into the stratosphere where they are broken down by ultraviolet rays from the Sun. They then give out chlorine, a gas which speeds up the rate at which ozone is destroyed.

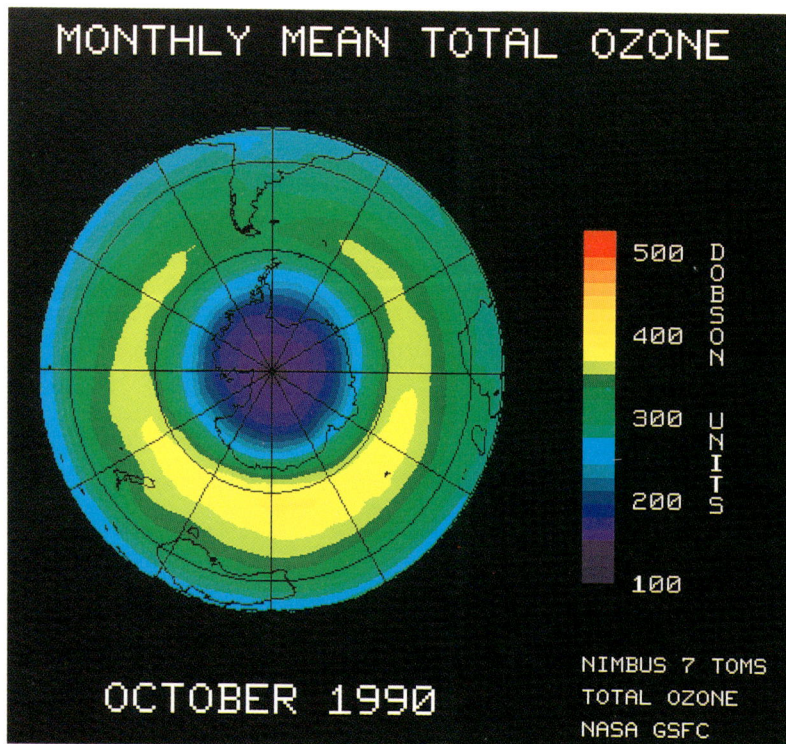

A satellite map showing a large hole in the ozone layer over Antarctica. The hole was caused by pollution of the atmosphere by chlorofluorocarbons (CFCs), used in aerosols and refrigerants. The hole was first seen in 1979 and is growing larger every year. It is visible here as the purple-blue oval covering most of Antarctica (outlined in black).

The ozone layer acts as a shield, protecting us from the harmful ultraviolet rays of the Sun. If the ozone layer is damaged, a harmful wave of ultraviolet light (UV-B) reaches the Earth's surface. This causes skin cancer, eye and skin disorders, and makes people more likely to catch diseases such as herpes (a painful skin disease).

UV-B does not only affect humans. It can penetrate up to 20 m into the ocean where, scientists say, it is killing phytoplankton, an organism essential to the food chain in the sea. Trees and plants are also sensitive to UV-B, particularly peas, melons and mustard.

In the northern parts of the Earth, scientists say there has been a 6-8 per cent loss of ozone in the upper atmosphere. They say that a steady 10 per cent loss would lead to 300,000 more cases of skin cancer a year, and 1,600,000 more cases of cataracts.

The nations of the world have taken this threat quite seriously. In 1987, many countries signed the Montreal Protocol on Substances that Deplete the Ozone Layer, agreeing to limit the production of the harmful chemicals. The Protocol has been updated regularly, so that now eighty-six countries have agreed to stop making CFCs by the end of 1995. HCFCs will not disappear until 2030. Halons are to go in 1994 and methyl chloroform, used in dry cleaning, by 2005.

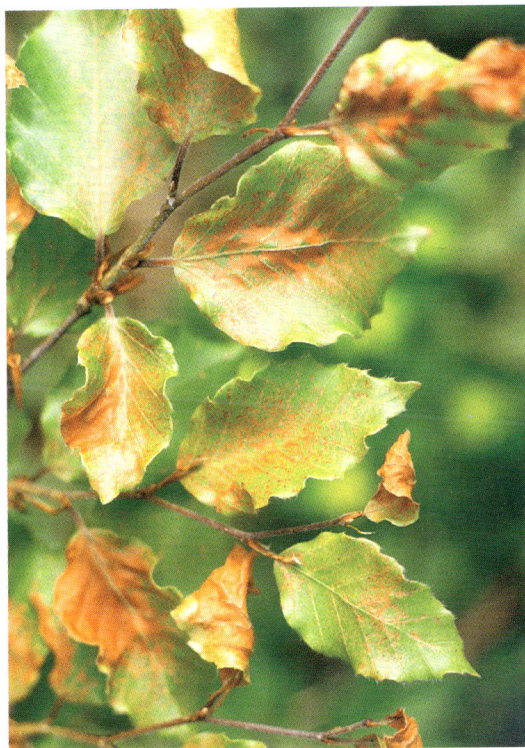

Harmful ultraviolet rays from the Sun, normally shielded by the ozone layer, have turned the leaves brown on this Swiss beech tree.

Environmental groups, however, are calling for an immediate and total ban on all chemicals that harm the ozone layer. Every five years' delay adds eighteen years to the time it will take the ozone layer to recover, they say. Left alone, the ozone layer would regenerate (renew itself). But without a stronger stand by governments, it seems as though we will all have to suffer the horrible consequences of the destruction of the ozone layer for some years to come.

4

Safe water

AFTER air, water is the most important element for human's and, indeed, for the Earth's survival. Three-quarters of the world's surface is covered in water, but less than one-hundredth of the water is suitable for people to drink. Unfortunately, the usable water is not evenly distributed around the world. This means that almost half the world's population, which is about 2 billion people, do not have safe water or even the most basic toilet facilities.

This lack of clean water leads to dreadful diseases. Drinking dirty water infects people with deadly parasites and illnesses such as typhoid or cholera. Water-related diseases kill approximately 25,000 children a day.

More than half the people in the world do not have access to clean, safe water. Most of these people live in developing countries, where the job of collecting water is usually performed by women. Often, the women have to walk for hours to fetch the water.

Collecting water in developing countries is often an extremely difficult task, and one almost always performed by women. The nearest supply is often many kilometres away, and women walk for hours to fetch the water.

There are many schemes being undertaken throughout the world by governments, charities, and local people to improve the supplies of clean water. Most of the projects are suited to the communities where they are needed. These include gravity-fed wells, which are simple pipelines bringing water from a spring to a village, and hand-drilled tube-wells fitted with hand-pumps. Such schemes can make a huge difference to communities. Erika Ngalya lives in Sagara, a village in the dry Dodoma region of Kenya. Recently, a tube-well was dug in Erika's village. She explains, 'I used to go to our spring in the hills at 6 o'clock in the morning and was not home until midday. In the dry season I was as late as 3 or 4 o'clock in the afternoon. We were unable to keep our children and houses clean as we could only carry one bucket of water a day. Now, I only have to wait fifteen minutes to fetch water and I don't need to queue. I am free to farm more and my children wash regularly.'

It takes very little money to improve water supplies in many areas. For example, in Sierra Leone, a gravity-fed scheme to bring water to the heart of the community would cost between £20,000 and £30,000 and would serve 10-20,000 people. The United Nations estimates that it would take US $25 million a day to provide clean water throughout the world – just 10 per cent of what people in the world spend on cigarettes each day.

Women in the Philippines collecting water from a stand pipe in their village. The pipe was built with money and assistance from Oxfam, the international aid organization. Before, people in the village did not have running water and had to travel 40 km to the nearest water supply.

So, why is the money not being spent? In 1981, the United Nations announced the start of a 'Water Decade' which aimed to provide 'clean water and sanitation for everyone by 1990.' Yet, despite help from governments, organizations and local people, by 1990 there was about the same number of people without safe water as in 1981. This was partly because of population growth, and partly because governments did not put enough money into the scheme.

It is not only developing countries which suffer from a shortage of water.

The dry river bed that was once the River Darent in Kent. The river, like many others, ran dry because so much water was taken out of it.

Although the shortage in other countries is nowhere near as serious, the once plentiful supplies are now running out. One of the reasons for this is over-extraction (too much water is taken out of rivers etc). Rivers are beginning to run dry because so much water is being taken out of them. The River Darent in England, for example, has completely disappeared.

A lot of drinking water comes from sources under the ground. It is known as groundwater. Groundwater is formed when rain seeps through the soil and is held in water-bearing rocks. A large amount of groundwater is called an aquifer. Heavily populated countries are pumping so much water out of their aquifers that the water table, the level of water below the ground, is dropping. In the USA, the vast Ogallala aquifer, which lies under eight of the states of the Great Plains, is being pumped out so fast that the water table is dropping by up to 1 m a year. Aquifers in China and India are showing similar falls.

It is not only over-extraction which is reducing the supplies of water. Many aquifers have been ruined by pollution. In rural areas, chemicals from pesticides and nitrates from fertilizers seep through the soil and into the groundwater. Nitrates move through the soil at a rate of about 90 cm a year.

A flock of seagulls circles over bales of rubbish at a landfill site in Wales. They are looking for bits of food.

More pollution of groundwater occurs round landfill sites, the huge tips where we dump much of the rubbish from our homes. The rubbish rots under the ground, creating methane gas and many other chemicals. Rain and liquids in the landfill site mix with the other chemicals to create a poisonous fluid called leachate. This can then seep through the soil into the water supply.

In San José in California, local people noticed a sudden rise in the number of miscarriages (women losing unborn babies) and babies born with disabilities in a small area of the town. They discovered that dangerous chemicals had leaked into the town's water supply from an underground storage tank at a nearby company. Later, the authorities tested seventy-nine companies and found sixty-five had dangerous chemicals stored underground.

A lot of our water also comes from rivers and streams, which are also polluted. In Poland, at least half the river water is too polluted even for industrial use. In Malaysia, more than forty major rivers are so contaminated that they have almost no fish or animals left in them.

This pollution is not irreversible. Lake Erie, one of the Great Lakes in Canada, was once completely dead.

Pollution had killed all the fish and plants in Lake Erie, one of the Great Lakes in Canada. Now, thanks to anti-pollution measures, there is life in Lake Erie again.

Thanks to anti-pollution measures it is now returning to life, although scientists say that at the present rate it will take another seventy-five years to clean it up completely.

More than 200 large dams are built every year. It is believed that by the end of the twentieth century, almost two-thirds of all the world's rivers will have been dammed. Damming changes the channel of the river. This can destroy fisheries, lead to silting up of water supplies and increase the amount of salt in previously fresh water.

We are not only threatening our groundwater and our rivers, however.

The seas and oceans are vast resources of food, fuel in the forms of gas and oil, minerals and chemicals. They play major roles in transport, defence, communications and recreation and they influence climate. Yet we take very little care of them, pouring 22 billion tonnes of pollution into seas and oceans every year. Because of the size of seas and oceans, the effects of the pollution have so far been kept under control, but this cannot last forever.

The pollution starts at the coast, either from industries pumping waste directly into the sea, or from rivers carrying the pollution to the sea. Italy's River Po carries 230 tonnes of arsenic, 18,000 tonnes of phosphates and 135,000 tonnes of nitrates into the Adriatic Sea.

Nuclear power stations are often built by the sea so they can use the water for cooling. The water used for cooling becomes slightly radioactive and is pumped back into the sea. In the UK, the Sellafield nuclear plant reprocesses nuclear waste from Japan and most of Europe. The liquid nuclear waste from Sellafield is piped into the Irish Sea, making it the most radioactive sea in the world, according to the British Ministry of Agriculture, Fisheries and Food. Many fish have been found suffering from cancers and their young are born severely deformed.

Another problem is caused by the phosphates from washing powders and the nitrates from fertilizers. These are very rich nitrogen compounds and act like fertilizer in the sea. Millions of algae (a type of seaweed) grow, covering the water with red, brown, blue or green algal bloom. When the algae die they sink to the bottom and rot. This process uses up a lot of oxygen – oxygen the fish and other plants need to grow. This is called eutrophication or over-nourishment. Eutrophication has killed many fish in the shallow waters off the Danish, German and Dutch coasts. It also affects rivers and lakes in many countries.

Raw, untreated sewage pours into the sea from a low tunnel near the main holiday beach in Torquay, on the south coast of England.

Shipping also poses a threat to our seas and oceans. A chemical that is used to keep ships' bottoms free of barnacles and weeds often leaks into the sea killing many fish and plants.

Oil spills pose the most serious problems. The worst oil spill was caused by the accident to the oil tanker, the *Exxon Valdez*. The tanker ran aground in Alaska in 1989, affecting 1,300 km of coast and 4,800 sq km of water. Tens of thousands of sea birds and animals died as a result.

So what can be done? Water is a world resource needing world attention. Individual countries do what they can to make sure their citizens have

Using high-power water jets to clean up the oil spill from the Exxon Valdez *in Alaska.*

clean, fresh water. The government of Switzerland banned phosphates because it was worried about eutrophication in its lakes. The European Commission laid down sixty quality standards for drinking water, which member states always break. Tougher laws, and a commitment to making sure they are upheld, are needed now.

Meanwhile, we can all help. We must think about what we flush down our drains and toilets, use phosphate-free washing powders and generally reduce the amount of water we use.

5

Transport

CARS allow us to live long distances from work, visit faraway places, expand our businesses, our leisure and our knowledge. But the benefits of using cars have to be weighed against the disadvantages.

Cars are not only the largest source of air pollution, but they also pollute water supplies and the countryside, and they are directly responsible for killing people. Every year, 265,000 people are killed and 10 million are injured on the roads world-wide.

To improve our traffic flow we build more roads, but these fill up almost as soon as they are built. In London, traffic during the rush hour moves at just 18 kph. In fact, London holds the record for the longest traffic jam – 53 km.

Destroying old or unwanted cars also harms the environment. Every year European drivers scrap 13 million cars. In the UK, more than 30 million tyres are scrapped every year, of which only one-sixth are recycled. The rest

Using a fire-fighting spray to put out smouldering tyres at the 'Tyre King' dump in Ontario, Canada. It would have been much less harmful to the environment if the tyres had been recycled.

About 70 per cent of this typical family car could be recycled.

are dumped, many in landfill sites, but most in vast piles often consisting of as many as 10 million tyres. These dumps frequently catch fire, releasing large quantities of poisonous fumes into the air, as well as oil into the groundwater. The fires are extremely difficult to put out.

One solution is more effective recycling. In Germany, part of the cost of every tyre is set aside to be spent on recycling.

About 128 million litres of motor oil are flushed into rivers and streams in the UK every year. Again this could be, and in a few places is, recycled. But no country has yet developed a national recycling scheme for unwanted car parts.

Yet about 70 per cent of a typical family car could be recycled easily. The rest, a mixture of almost 20,000 parts, made of plastics, glass, rubber and fibre, is not so easy to recycle. In Germany, some manufacturers are seeking to overcome this problem by making car parts more easily recyclable. Mercedes are making the glove compartments in their saloons (four-door cars) from papier mâché made of recycled newspapers. BMW collects damaged bumpers, which are sent to Germany to be ground down and reused as boot linings and floor mats.

If enough effort and investment were made, almost all the parts of a car could be recycled. But this will only happen if the motor industry as a whole agrees to tackle the problem and sets up a series of national recycling centres used by all the car companies.

This would begin to solve the problems of waste from cars, but not the problem of pollution from cars still on the road. The only real solution to this is to have fewer cars.

If public transport is to lure people out of their cars on to buses and trains, the services must go where people want to go and when they want to go. It must also be cheaper to use public transport than to run a car. Public transport, of whatever form, uses less fuel per passenger than private vehicles and so causes much less pollution.

A trolley which carries passengers to different parts of the city of San Diego, California. The trolley system has proved very popular and successful with passengers. So popular, in fact, that the system has been expanded and trolleys now run in the suburbs of the city.

Some cities are increasing their levels of public transport. Since 1970, twenty-one large cities have built Metro systems. In California, the highly successful trolley network in San Diego has been expanded, and an extensive new rail system is being built in Los Angeles.

The only totally pollution-free way to travel is by bicycle or on foot. But people need to be encouraged to return to pedal power or to be pedestrians. The authorities in Harare, the capital of Zimbabwe, take this need for encouragement seriously. The civil service offers its employees low-cost loans to buy bicycles. Shop-keepers are obliged by law to provide special parking bays for the bicycles, and cycle lanes make travelling much safer.

Most cities now also cater for pedestrians with pedestrian-only zones. But, too often, pedestrians have to share these streets with buses, taxis and large delivery lorries. To persuade people to walk rather than use cars, it is important to make them feel safe and comfortable (see chapter 6).

The safest way to travel as a passenger is by aeroplane. But the latest scientific evidence points to aircraft as a major pollutant of the atmosphere. In Europe, aircraft contribute eight times as much to the greenhouse effect as cars. Nitrogen oxides make up two-thirds of the fumes given off by an aeroplane. Nitrogen reacts with hydrocarbons in the sunlight to produce ozone, which, at the height aeroplanes fly, is a greenhouse gas.

Air travel also harms the environment by causing a great deal of noise pollution (see chapter 8) and, when building a new airport, by destroying often unique natural sites.

There is a great need for countries to develop a properly planned transport system to take into account the needs of people and the needs of the environment. We, as transport users, should be more responsible. We should walk, cycle or use public transport as often as possible.

An aeroplane takes off from La Guardia airport in New York. Aeroplanes are considered to be major causes of pollution. In fact, statistics show that, in Europe, aeroplanes contribute eight times as much to the greenhouse effect as cars.

6

Safe cities

MOST of the people in the world live in cities. In 1980 there were thirty-eight cities with more than 4 million people living in them. By the year 2000 that number is expected to have grown to 86 million.

Cities should be lively and interesting places to live. With lots of people, leisure facilities, businesses and industries, life should be quite easy. Instead, many cities breed crime, vandalism, stress and loneliness. This is usually the fault of poor planning. Very few cities have been planned around the people who live in them. They have grown up haphazardly, and such planning as does occur usually caters for the needs of industries and businesses.

Cities are like magnets. People are drawn to cities in search of jobs and better lives. They are often disappointed. The populations of many, especially newer, cities are swelling at an enormous rate. It is estimated that 1,000 people arrive in Mexico City every day. There are neither the houses nor the roads, electricity, drains or water supplies, to support them. In 1993 Mexico City had a population of 18-20 million people. By 2000 it is expected to be the largest city in the world with 31 million people.

Mexico City is thought to be one of the most densely populated cities in the world. There is a severe problem of overcrowding in the city, and many people have to live in makeshift slums.

A large number of the people who go to live in cities like Mexico City end up in shanty towns, built, often illegally, on infertile, dangerous land the rich do not want to build on. They live in packing-cases, drain pipes, anything they can turn into shelters. The shanty towns usually do not have electricity or running water.

As cities develop, much of the surrounding countryside is destroyed. Water is drained, fuel supplies are used up, and thousands of tonnes of sewage and refuse are dumped, until the countryside is unfit for people to live in.

It is not only the poorest areas of cities that suffer, however. Wealthier areas are by no means free from problems. In the 1970s and 1980s, city planners believed they were creating good environments for residents by building large shopping centres, industrial estates, huge schools and vast housing estates. But this means very few destinations are within walking distance and people do not meet. Without a strong, stable social structure communities are broken up.

An aerial view of a residential area on the outskirts of London.

The winding, twisting freeway in downtown Los Angeles, California.

It is important that city centres have a mixture of uses. In Pakistan there is a programme for developing the city centre of Karachi. The programme is called Metroville. It enables people to build their own houses within walking distance of their jobs. Half of all new flats in Toronto, Canada are built within walking distance of the rapid rail system. Ninety per cent of all new offices have to be next to railway stations or at one of three other locations.

There is still a need for green, open spaces with trees, flowers and shrubs. Unfortunately, in too many cities the need for more roads to carry the increasing number of cars has overwhelmed people's need for space.

Few cities address the needs of pedestrians and cyclists. Los Angeles, for example, has two-thirds of its urban space paved over for vehicles.

When all the surface space has been given over to cars, developers go overhead or underground – flyovers, underpasses and tunnels. In Yokohama, in Japan, there is even a floating car-park in the local bay.

Some cities are trying to undo the damage caused by road traffic. They are trying to turn streets into proper, attractive places rather than just vehicle routes. In 1988, the city centre in Florence, Italy, became open to pedestrians only, after years of motorist madness.

One of the most successful traffic calming schemes was started in the Netherlands more than twenty years ago. The Dutch developed a method which is called 'Woonerf' or 'living yard'. It involves planting trees and shrubs in the roads and building humps and chicanes so that cars have to travel very slowly and carefully. Germany has a similar scheme called 'Verkehrsbernhigung'.

Not all schemes to reduce traffic are successful. The Greek government announced that, in Athens, drivers with odd-numbered licence plates would drive on alternate days to those with even-numbered plates. Instead of halving the number of cars on the roads as intended, it led to many people buying two cars, one with odd- and the other with even-numbered plates.

It is not only the overall planning of a city which is important for the people living there. The type of housing also has an important effect on community life. People are often not considered by large developers, which aim to build as many houses as cheaply as possible.

The 'Woonerf' in Amsterdam, the Netherlands, has been made into a residential area. Now people have priority over all vehicles, the drivers of which have been forced to travel more slowly.

After the Second World War in Europe (1939-45), huge, high-rise blocks of flats were built in many of those cities which had been badly affected. In other cities, high-rise flats were built to replace slums. Many social problems, such as vandalism, crime and mental illness, especially among women, resulted.

It was found that a few quite simple measures would help to lessen some of these problems: staircases instead of balconies and walkways; special places for drying clothes so they are not draped all over the flats; separate front doors for every home, and gardens wherever possible.

A cluster of tower blocks in the Possil Park estate in Glasgow, Scotland. The high-rise flats were built to replace slums after the Second World War. However, they have become slums once again.

The authorities in Puerto Rico found their first five estates of flats bred so many problems, that they abandoned them for self-help housing schemes.

A properly planned city brings benefits to a country in a variety of ways. It reduces pollution, cuts crime, vandalism and many social ills, and becomes a source of pride to the people who live in it.

7

The countryside

THE countryside is under threat. Pollution, development and farming are combining to destroy some of the most beautiful natural places on the Earth.

We are also destroying land which provides jobs for millions of people and produces food for billions more. Often, it is the very efforts to improve the agricultural industry which ruin the land on which it depends.

Over the last fifty years, farmers have removed hedges and cut down trees to make larger fields. This makes it easier for large agricultural machinery to be used One of the results of this is a loss of topsoil. With no hedges to

Part of the 'great green wall', the San Bei forest belt, which was built in China to stabilize the badly eroded uplands and to stop the forest encroaching on land used for crops.

hold it in place, the topsoil is exposed and blows away or washes into nearby rivers. It takes between 500 and 1000 years to make 1 cm of topsoil and 20 cm are needed to grow food. Every year, 6.2 million hectares of topsoil are lost, an area twice the size of Belgium.

When the topsoil has been lost, the land that is left is like a desert. This is called desertification. Vast areas of land in Australia, South and North America are threatened with desertification. Unless there are big changes in farming practices, 355,000 million tonnes of topsoil will be eroded and 2,912,000 sq km of desert will be formed by the year 2000.

The loss of topsoil can be reversed. In China, farmers planted thousands of trees to form 'a great green wall', the San Bei forest belt, to stabilize the badly eroded uplands. Grain harvests have improved by 13 per cent as a result. In Rajesthan in India, and in parts of West Africa, acacia trees were planted to retain the soil. In Burkina Faso, simple lines of stones were placed in the fields to trap the earth.

Desertification has also occurred in areas where groundwater has been pumped out to use for irrigation. Badly designed irrigation schemes dry out the land, waste water, wash nutrients from the soil and can lead to harmful levels of salt building up on the land.

Better systems of irrigation help soil. So, too, does more mixed farming which means more animal dung going into the soil. Animal dung is a good, natural fertilizer. The old-fashioned method of crop rotation, which leaves fields without crops for one out of every two or three years, also improves the quality of soil.

Unfortunately, many farmers prefer to use more and more chemical fertilizers to increase their crop production. They also spray crops with pesticides. These result in water and soil polluted with nitrates and other chemicals (see chapter 4).

Deforestation in the Brazilian rainforests caused an average of one tribe of people a year to be wiped out between 1900 and 1970.

In many areas of the world, forests are being cut down to make way for cattle-ranching, mining, dam-building and road construction. This poses a number of threats to the environment. Not only is it contributing to global warming, but it is also killing many animals and plants. The world's forests cover about one-third of all land and support more than two-thirds of plant and animal species. It is feared that by 2000, we could have lost one-fifth of the world's species.

Deforestation is also destroying people's lives. In Brazil, an average of one tribe of people died out each year between 1900 and 1970. For the tribes which remain, the loss of forests traps them in what is called 'the poor person's energy crisis'. They cannot find enough fuel to cook their food. They have to walk long distances to collect enough wood to cook. This means they cook less often and when they do they cook more grain. Grain is less nutritious than the traditional pulses, but cooks more quickly and so uses less fuel. Some farming communities now burn dung instead of wood, which means it is not returned to the earth where it would enrich the soil.

Forests are not the only habitat being destroyed. The world's wetlands are home to vast numbers of plants, birds and insects, which cannot survive in any other type of environment. But

An aerial view of the world's largest dam site at Itaipu, Brazil. The Itaipu Dam is expected to produce as much electricity as ten nuclear power stations.

the wetlands are being drained to make way for building developments and many species have been lost.

Other parts of the countryside are being destroyed by developers. As cities grow, the resources of the surrounding countryside are used up. But as the demand for housing grows, so does the need for land on which to build. Once again, a balance has to be struck between the needs of people and the needs of the environment.

In developing countries, big dams are extremely fashionable and getting bigger all the time. The Itaipu Dam, on the borders of Paraguay and Brazil, is built of enough concrete to pave a motorway stretching from Paris to the Persian Gulf. Itaipu is expected to produce as much electricity as ten nuclear power stations. The water collected can also be used to irrigate crops, and the dam will, hopefully, be a great tourist attraction.

However, the Itaipu Dam also has many environmental disadvantages. Huge sections of forest had to be cleared to build it and even more were flooded afterwards. Thousands of plants and animals were destroyed. Thousands of people, mostly peasant farmers, had to give up their homes and move to the shanty towns in near-by cities.

Around 60 per cent of all the rivers in the world are now dammed. One of the most recent is the Danube, despite a long campaign by environmentalists against the dam. They say it will mean the last wetland forest in Europe will dry out because the water has been diverted away from it. Some campaigns to stop dams being built have been successful, notably in Tasmania, where the Franklin River was to have been blocked, and in France where plans to dam the Loire, Europe's last 'wild river', were thwarted.

The opponents of the environmental campaigners say that the countryside cannot be kept as a picturesque, traditional landscape. They say it should be a working environment and must be profitable and productive. But a middle way has to be found if disaster is not to strike our countryside.

Plans to dam the beautiful River Loire in France were thwarted by environmentalists keen to preserve Europe's last 'wild river'.

8

A safe environment

MANY of the problems we have looked at have concerned the world's environment. But many environmental issues arise in your own home, where you should be able to feel as comfortable and safe as possible. Yet, it is in your home where most accidents occur. In the UK, as many people die from accidents in the home as on the roads, and many more are injured.

To try to cut down the number of accidents, the governments of many countries have passed strict laws about the safety standards of appliances, furniture, tools and toys. Unfortunately, not all countries have the same standards and too often companies are able to sell products with lower safety standards to countries with more relaxed rules.

Many accidents also occur at work. Again, some countries have strict rules about safety in the workplace. However, small companies often have a more relaxed attitude to safety. Governments must have health and safety and environmental health inspectors to keep a check on companies.

One of the most serious problems affecting people both at home and at work is noise. People have more and noisier possessions. Traffic, stereo equipment, lawnmowers, barking dogs and aeroplanes all create an often unbearable level of noise.

Noise causes physical and mental stress. People who have to put up with long periods of loud noise can suffer heart disease, stomach disorders, problems with blood circulation and deafness. Animals which are made to listen to loud noise become moody, depressed and violent. Indeed, some people who live next to neighbours with noisy stereo systems, or who are plagued by burglar or car alarms constantly ringing, have themselves been driven to acts of violence.

In France, the city of Lille has had a noise reduction policy for more than twenty years. Roads in the old part of the city have been resurfaced and anti-noise screens have been put up along motorways. The oldest public sector housing has been sound-proofed, as have all the major public buildings, such as hospitals and schools.

Imagine the noise pollution suffered by people living in these houses near Heathrow Airport, London.

The authorities in Lille discovered that their school canteens were particularly noisy with decibel levels of 85 (anything above 80 decibels is dangerous). Children found it hard to talk to each other at meal times and were becoming irritable, aggressive, tired and complained of headaches and loss of appetite.

Putting in carpets to reduce the noise was not possible because of the problems of cleaning. Instead, sound-absorbent materials for ceilings, panels and partitions were fitted. Partitions were put between the tables, and chairs with rubber-tipped legs were provided. These simple, inexpensive measures made a huge difference to the noise levels.

Transport noise is the main nuisance in many towns. Noise affects people's health and, because of the vibrations it causes, it damages buildings and roads too. Germany has put the cost of damage caused by transport noise at DM 33 billion. In the USA, 5 million people have to put up with road traffic noise of 65 decibels or more. There are measures that can reduce this level of noise; improving road surfaces, putting up anti-noise barriers and changing the behaviour of drivers. In some states in Australia, police fine drivers of noisy vehicles.

People also want to feel safe in their environment. In most cities all over the world, there is a growing problem with violent crime. Research has shown that feelings of alienation, poverty, overcrowding and unemployment all contribute to high levels of violence.

But these are problems that can only be overcome by radical political decisions and changes in economic policies. There are short-term measures that can be taken to combat violence, such as better street lighting, safer housing and wider streets.

The long-term measures will probably only come when governments are prepared to take more radical steps to deal with all the world's problems. The threats facing the environment could be cured almost overnight, if we did not have to balance the needs of people against the needs of the environment. It is true that often the demands of industry seem to outweigh the needs of people and planet alike. But industry does provide jobs without which people could not survive. Governments have very difficult choices to make.

What has been highlighted throughout this book is the lack of any kind of joint effort by governments to combat the dangers that are facing all of us,

A backstreet of Chicago, USA. There is no street lighting in the area, which, not surprisingly, is a haven for muggers.

We must all help to protect the environment so that it can be enjoyed by future generations.

wherever we live. It is not until national considerations are put to one side that countries will really tackle global warming, or acid rain, or population growth. It is going to take a radical re-think by governments before this can happen. Let us not forget that many governments are only in place because people have voted for them. If we, the voters, changed our attitudes towards the environment we could change the people in power.

Until then it could not be said that we have many rights to a clean, safe environment. However, we do have a lot of responsibilities; responsibility for saving valuable resources; for not using products which contribute to the destruction of the environment; for caring more about all animals and humans. A sign of hope is the number of young people who are actively involved in the environmental movement. With a more aware younger generation poised to take over running the world, with luck the balance will swing in favour of the environment. The planet might yet be saved.

Glossary

Algae Seaweed and other weeds that live in water.

Atmosphere The mixture of gases that surrounds the Earth. The two main gases are oxygen and nitrogen.

Carbon dioxide A gas produced when we breathe out and when fuels like coal, gas or oil are burned.

Carbon monoxide A very poisonous gas, which has no colour or smell. It is found in the fumes of car exhausts.

Catalytic converter A device fitted in car exhausts which turns most of the posionous fumes into carbon dioxide, nitrogen and water.

Combined Heat and Power (CHP) station Here, heat is used to produce steam to drive turbines, which generate electricity. The heat from the steam is piped to nearby homes and factories, instead of being wasted as in a conventional power station.

Communities Groups of people who live in one place.

Contaminated Polluted or made dirty.

Famine When there is no, or very little, food in an area or country.

Insulate To keep things warm by covering them with thick material. Insulation can save energy – thick material used to cover heating pipes or boilers stops heat from escaping.

Nitrogen A gas which makes up almost 80 per cent of the air we breathe.

Nitrogen oxides Polluting gases formed from nitrogen in the air. They are produced when fossil fuels are burned.

Radiation Dangerous rays of energy, which are produced by the fuel in nuclear power stations.

Rainforest A dense type of forest found in tropical areas of the world.

Sanitation The use of proper, hygienic methods which are important for good health.

Sewage Waste from our toilets.

Stratosphere An upper layer of the atmosphere, many kilometres above the Earth's surface.

Ultraviolet rays Invisible rays of light from the Sun.

Ventilation system A system whereby fresh air is circulated around a building and much stale air out of it.

Further reading

Acid Rain by John Baines (Wayland, 1989)

Acid Rain by Tony Hare (Franklin Watts, 1990)

Atlas of the Environment by Geoffrey Lean, Don Hinrichsen and Adam Markham (Hutchinson, 1990)

Conserving Our World series (Wayland, 1989-90)

Green Detective series (Wayland, 1990)

Green Energy: A Non-Nuclear Response to the Greenhouse Effect by Dave Toke (Greenprint, 1990)

Human Rights by David Selby (Cambridge University Press, 1987)

Human Rights by Jane Sherwin (Wayland, 1989)

Human Rights: Food by Scarlett MccGwire (Wayland, 1993)

1001 Ways to Save the Planet by Bernadette Vallely (Penguin, 1990)

Only One Earth by Lloyd Timberlake (BBC/Earthscan)

State of the World 1991 by Lester R Brown (Earthscan)

The Dying Sea by Michael Bright (Franklin Watts, 1988)

Utopia on Trial by Alice Coleman (Hilary Shipman, 1985)

Women and the Environment in the Third World by Irene Dankelman and Joan Davidson (Earthscan, 1987)

Useful addresses

British Institute of Human Rights
King's College, London
Faculty of Law
The Strand
London WC2R 2LS

European Commission of Human Rights
Conseil De L'Europe
Boite Postale 431 R6
F-67006 Strasbourg Cedex
France

International Institute of Human Rights
1 Quai Lezay-Marnesia
F-67000 Strasbourg
France

United Nations Commission on Human Rights
Palais Des Nations
CH-1211 Geneva 10
Switzerland

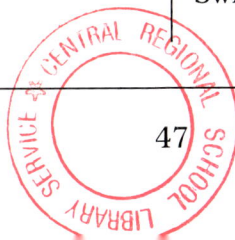

CENTRAL REGIONAL SCHOOL LIBRARY SERVICE

Index

EASTER

A STORY AND

ACTIVITY BOOK

Written by

Wendy Hobson

Illustrated by

Rhian Nest James

Consultant:

Beryl Goodland

Macdonald

22040710G

CONTENTS

236427

CLACKMANNAN
DISTRICT LIBRARY

22040710G